ESAU C.

# THE FORBIDDEN LIBRARY

## VOLUME 1

# 13 SCARY STORIES
## THAT SHOULD NEVER BE TOLD

TO YOU,
IF YOU MANAGE TO
SURVIVE READING
ALL 13 STORIES...

ISBN: 9798339991540
Imprint: Independently published

# Contents

# PREPARE YOURSELF, BRAVE READERS!

Before diving into these eerie tales, arm yourself with the art of chilling storytelling. Follow these tips as you read the stories out loud to ensure a truly haunting experience. You'll have your audience jumping at every creak and shadow.
Let's make the dark a bit scarier tonight.

Read on and master the craft of fear!

**Dim the Lights:** Create a shadowy atmosphere with dim lights or read by flashlight to set the mood.

**Eerie Music:** Play some eerie music quietly in the background (Try playing the sounds of planets)

**Start Slow:** Begin reading slowly to draw listeners in.

**Secretive Tone:** Remember you're sharing a forbidden story that should never be told. Read it like you don't want anyone catching you sharing it.

**Draw Out Words:** Especially eerie words, like "daaaark" and "shadoooows," to heighten suspense.

**Pause for Tension:** After key moments, pause just long enough for everyone to feel the chill creeping in.

**Variable Speed:** Speed up during tense moments as the terror reveals itself.

**Eerie Ending:** Slow down again when you reach the last few words or sentences. On the very last word, let your voice trail off to create an eerie, unfinished feeling.

# 1
# AN OPEN BOOK

Scott loved scary stories. He read every scary book he could get his hands on. But none of them really scared him before. That's what he told his friend Owen one day at the library.

"I've read all the scary books here," Scott bragged, "None of them scared me."

"Is that so?" Asked the old librarian as she came around the corner. "I might have something hidden away in the back that might interest you."

Scott and Owen followed the old librarian to a dark corner in the back of the library, where she unlocked an old cabinet. Inside was a dusty, old book with a black leather cover.

Scott felt a chill as he looked at the book. This has to be a terrifying book, he thought.

Owen looked uneasy. "There's something wrong about that book," he said. "I don't think you should take it."

But Scott didn't listen. "Just because you're too scared of it doesn't mean I am."

Owen shook his head and left as the librarian handed the book to Scott. He took it, but she didn't let it go.

"I have to warn you." The old librarian leaned down closer to Scott. "This book might be too scary for you. Are you sure you want to take it?"

When Scott touched the book, the dark corner of the library seemed to grow darker.

"Yes," Scott said, determined. "It can't be that

scary."

The old librarian let go of the book and smiled. "I suppose you'll have to let me know when you return it."

Scott nodded and hurried home.

That night, he got into bed and began to read.

'There once was a boy who asked a librarian for a terrifying book.'

A shiver ran down Scott's spine.

'The librarian took him to a dark corner of the library. She showed him an old book. She warned the boy about the book, but he foolishly took it home anyway.'

Goosebumps rose on Scott's arms, but he continued reading.

'That night, the boy sat in his bed and opened the book. He began to read the first page. As he did, he got an awful feeling. The boy knew something terrible would happen if he kept reading. He knew it was his last chance to stop before it was too late. His hand trembled as he held the corner, still deciding to turn the page.'

That was the end of the first page. Scott's hand trembled as he held the page, ready to turn it.

Owen was right. There was something wrong with the book. The story kept describing everything Scott was doing! For the first time, he really was scared. But he had to know what was going to happen.

Scott turned the page.

'The boy turned the page, unable to stop reading. The room was dark. The only light came from a small bedside lamp. The light cast a shadow of the boy on the wall behind him. But the boy couldn't see the shadow even when it began to move on its own. The shadow's arms reached out towards the boy.'

Scott paused.

The hair on the back of his neck rose.

He could feel something watching him.

Scott spun around. There was nothing there but his own normal shadow.

Scott tried to laugh, but the sound caught in his throat. You're being silly, he told himself; it was just a book.

Nervously, he turned back to the story.

'The boy felt something watching him. But when he turned around, all he saw was his own normal shadow. The boy told himself it was only the book. But deep down, he knew he was wrong. Behind him, the shadow began to move again, preparing to strike. But the boy didn't look.'

Scott yawned and rubbed his eyes.

'The boy's eyes began to droop. It was too hard to stay awake.'

Scott couldn't even finish the following sentence before he fell asleep.

'As soon as Scott nodded off to sleep, the shadow suddenly—'

It was late at night, but the old librarian sat at her desk, waiting. All the lights were out in the library except the small desk lamp beside her.

She knew it wouldn't be long now. She heard the library door open but didn't bother looking up. She knew who it was.

She heard footsteps approaching. From out of the shadows, a child-sized figure handed her a book. The old librarian took it. With a smile, she skimmed through the first pages. She stopped when they turned blank.

The old librarian shook her head sadly, "So many empty pages left to fill."

The shadowy, child-sized figure said nothing.

"Still," the old librarian said. "We're off to a good start, aren't we?"

The shadowy, child-sized figure said nothing.

The old librarian looked down at the shadowy figure.

"No, I suppose you wouldn't think so, would you?" The old librarian grinned wickedly. "It's not a good start at all. It's a horrible one!"

And with that, the old librarian cackled gleefully and snapped the book shut.

# 2

# THE CRAWLING
# FINGER

In a small, quiet house, there was a boy named Dean.

His room was cozy, with toy cars and colorful posters. It had all sorts of things that belonged in a child's bedroom. But one night, something strange happened. Something appeared that didn't belong.

Dean heard something scratching in the wall. He sat up, and from the moon's faint light, he saw a small hole in the wall.

Then suddenly, flop!

Something fell out of the hole onto the floor.

It looked like a giant caterpillar crawling around. Dean crawled to the edge of his bed and looked down.

It wasn't a caterpillar; it was a finger.

Dean jumped back under the covers. All night, he could hear the finger inching around and scratching at the floor.

In the morning, he told his mom. They went back upstairs, but the hole in the wall was gone. She told Dean it was just his imagination.

The next night, the scratching sound returned. Terrified, Dean watched as TWO fingers fell out of the hole and onto the floor.

Flop! Flop!

They began to crawl around.

In the morning, the hole had disappeared, and so had the fingers.

The next night, the hole reappeared; this time, THREE fingers fell onto the floor.

Flop! Flop! Flop!

And the next night, FOUR fingers!

Flop! Flop! Flop! Flop!

But on the fifth night, something different appeared.

Dean sat in his bed when he heard the scratching. It was louder than ever. He peeked out over the edge of his blanket. He watched as the hole appeared, growing larger and larger.

To the size of a quarter...

To the size of a ping-pong ball...

To the size of a softball...

Until finally...

FLOP!

Dean crept to the edge of the bed and looked down.

There on the floor was a severed hand, crawling toward his bedroom door.

But the door was closed. The hand began scratching frantically at the door, like a crazed cat desperate to get out.

Maybe, thought Dean, if I let it out, it'll go away.

As soon as he thought this, the hand stopped scratching. It turned to face Dean and waited.

Hesitantly, Dean crept out of bed. As soon as he cracked open the door, the hand scurried out into the hall.

The hand stopped at the foot of the stairs that led up to the attic. It turned back to face Dean, almost like it was waiting for him to follow.

Dean's heart pounded harder. He rarely went to the attic, which was dark and dusty. Old boxes and forgotten things were everywhere, covered in dust and spider webs. Dean was scared of spiders. The crawling hand looked like a giant spider in the darkness.

The hand began to crawl up the stairs, but Dean stood there terrified. He knew the attic door would be closed. Would the hand come back if it didn't get in? What would it do to him if he didn't help it? What would it do to him if he did?

The stairs creaked as Dean forced himself to follow the hand. At the top, he opened the attic door. The hand scurried past the old junk and dusty boxes and into the darkness.

Dean pulled the chain, and a dim fluorescent bulb lit the attic.

There was the hand, scratching at an old chest in the back.

Dean shuddered as he pushed through old hanging cobwebs. He opened the chest.

It was empty except for a rectangular package wrapped in tattered paper and twine.

The hand crawled up the side of the chest and pointed down at the package.

Slowly, Dean reached down and picked it up. The ancient twine snapped easily, and the paper crumbled away, revealing an old painting of a grizzly-looking pirate with a hook for a hand.

Dean felt a shiver down his spine as he looked into the pirate's cold gray eyes. They seemed to follow Dean.

Suddenly, the room turned cold.

The lightbulb rattled and burnt out, plunging the room into darkness. A haunting blue light filled

the attic. Dean heard the sound of a roaring sea wind and crashing waves.

"Arr!" shouted a coarse voice as a figure appeared before him. "I thank ye for finding my hand, matey!"

The ghostly form of the hook-handed pirate towered above him.

"Or perhaps," the ghost said with a cruel laugh, "Mayhap I'll just be takin' one of yar's!"

The ghost drew his sword and raised it high in the air.

Dean tried to dash for the attic door, but the ghost was faster.

The hook lashed out, snaring the back of Dean's pajama shirt. The ghostly pirate raised Dean into the air.

"What'll it be, matey?" The pirate roared. "Yer left, or yer right? Choose quick, or I'll be choosing for ye!"

This has to be a nightmare, Dean thought in his panic. He flailed and kicked and twisted, but there was no escape.

"My choice it be, then!" shouted the pirate with a dry, bony crackle.

In a flash, the sword plunged down!

# 3
# THE CURSE OF THE OLD TREE

A girl named Sofia loved playing in the woods behind her house. One day, she found a towering, old tree. The tree was gnarled and looked funny. It had a twisted, lumpy, gray trunk. There were three knotholes that almost looked like a face. But Sofia didn't care. The twisted trunk would make it easy for her to climb as high as she wanted.

Sofia gripped the bark and began climbing higher and higher. She passed the dark knotholes that looked like a face. Soon, she was in the highest branches she could reach and found a good place to sit.

When she looked down, she saw a boy staring up at her.

"You should stay away from this tree," the boy shouted. "It's cursed. There's something rotten inside it."

"There's no such thing as curses," she shouted back.

The boy said nothing. He just stared up at Sofia. She tried to glare back, but something bothered her about his eyes. It was light outside, but his eyes were dark. She had to look away. It was almost like he had no eyes at all.

When she looked down again, the boy was gone.

He's probably upset because he was too afraid to climb so high, Sofia thought.

But Sofia wasn't scared. She stayed in the tree for hours, enjoying the birds singing and the wind on her face. She watched the squirrels leaping and chasing each other through the branches. There was nothing wrong with the tree.

But it was starting to get dark, so Sofia climbed back down. She passed by the knotholes, and in the deepening shadows, the face looked more lonely than scary.

The tree's just sad that I have to go away, Sofia thought. When she reached the bottom, she waved goodbye. She promised to return the next day.

That night, Sofia had an awful dream. When she looked down at her hands, they looked

like tree bark, all rough and brown. She woke up scared but noticed her hands were normal.

It was just a bad dream, she thought.

While playing, Sofia touched the tree the next day and felt dizzy. She saw the world as if she was the face in the tree looking down at the world. She saw herself looking up at the tree. She shook her head, and everything was normal again.

"That was weird," she whispered.

She remembered the boy's words about

the curse as she began climbing the tree. She reached the knotholes that made the face. She felt like its eyes were watching her: lonely, sad, dark eyes.

She ignored them and kept climbing to the spot where she sat before.

Today, the clouds were darker. The wind blew colder. The song birds were gone. A group of black birds cawed and screeched at each other. Sofia didn't see any squirrels playing.

Maybe the boy was right. Maybe there was

something wrong with the tree.

Sofia began to climb down. But she didn't want to climb past the sad face. She never wanted to look at it again.

The wind picked up, tossing her hair in her eyes. The wind grew colder, and her fingers grew numb.

Suddenly, her foot slipped.

The branch she was holding snapped.

Frantically, she grasped at the twisted grey trunk, but the bark on that side crumbled away, and she fell into the tree's hollow center.

She stuck her hands and feet out, trying to slow her fall, but it wasn't any use. Deeper and deeper, she fell.

She landed with a hard thud.

She looked up at the hole she had fallen into high above her. She saw the three knotholes. From the inside, they looked like a pair of sinister eyes and a jagged mouth.

Sophia cried for help, but she doubted anyone would hear her.

She brushed the tears from her eyes.

There wasn't much room, and she scrambled around, trying to find a way out in the darkness. Maybe there was another rotten spot in the trunk, and she could break out.

Her hands brushed a pile of dried branches and old decaying leaves. A squirrel nest, she thought. Then she felt something else. A string?

She followed it with her hand and felt something strange and lumpy—a shoe!

The squirrels carried a shoe into their nest, she thought. Normally, the image of a squirrel carrying a shoe up a tree would've made her laugh. But not now. Not when she was trapped in the dark hollow tree. She was too scared to laugh.

Then, her hand felt something else strange, something hard and round.

Was it a giant egg?

"I told you to stay away," the boy whispered in her ear. "But at least now I won't have to rot alone…"

# 4
# DRIP, DRIP, DRIP

Ethan was nervous about visiting his Great Aunt Mabel's old house. As soon as he arrived, the old woman greeted him with a harsh glare. She gave him a strict warning not to touch anything. It was a large old house with that stuffy, old-house smell, filled with antique furniture, old paintings, knickknacks, sculptures, and lots of other strange objects from around the world.

During the day, it wasn't so bad. Ethan liked looking at all the curious things. But he was very careful not to touch anything. Still, Great Aunt Mabel kept watching him all day from across rooms or around corners. But at night, the floorboards creaked, and the lights were dim. All the strange things looked much spookier in the heavy shadows.

The room he slept in was no different.

There was an antique wardrobe carved with intricate birds, leaves, and flowers. But when the

lights were out, and only a bit of moonlight spilled through the window, the leaves looked like twisted, thorny vines, and the birds looked like evil eyes peeking out from behind them.

On the dresser was a music box with a man and a woman. They were dancing and wearing fancy old clothes and funny white wigs. But with the lights out, it cast a shadow on the wall that looked like a vampire in a billowing cloak with his arms reaching out.

Ethan knew it was just a shadow, but he

couldn't sleep with it there. He wanted to move it, but he'd been told not to touch anything. Nervously, he got out of bed and went to his parents' room down the hall.

He knocked on their door. They were both a bit annoyed at being woken up. But his father took Ethan back to his room. His father moved the music box to a shelf where the moonlight couldn't reach it.

Then, his father tucked him back into bed and was just leaving when Ethan asked him to do something about the wardrobe as well. His father found a spare blanket. Then he draped it over the wardrobe, covering the thorns and eyes.

"Anything else?" Asked his father with a yawn. "Should I cover up this old painting too?"

Ethan shook his head. The painting was of an old ship with full white sails on a calm blue ocean. It was one of the few things he liked about staying in the room.

"If anything else bothers you," his father said with a yawn. "I give you permission to move it or cover it up. Whatever. Just be careful, got it?"

Ethan nodded and thanked his father.

His father switched off the light and closed the door.

Ethan took another look around the dark room. No creepy eyes. No creepy shadows. Everything seemed fine until he saw the painting of the ship.

It looked crooked.

Usually, something like that wouldn't bother him, but that night it did. The more he tried to sleep, the stronger he felt the urge to fix it.

He pulled the covers aside and went over to the painting. Carefully, he held the frame by the corners and adjusted it slightly.

That's much better, he thought as he crawled back into bed. He rubbed his eyes with his hand. He felt something cold and wet: a drop of water.

He was too tired to wonder where it came from. But as he tried to sleep, he heard a noise.

Drip...

There it was again.

Drip...

And again.

Drip...

Over and over, he heard it.

Drip... Drip... Drip...

Ethan got up and checked the small bathroom attached to his room. He thought the faucet was leaky. But the sink was dry.

He went back to bed.

But the dripping sound continued.

Drip... Drip... Drip...

He tried to sleep but couldn't tune out the dripping noise. He tried to cover his head with the pillow but could still hear it.

If anything, it dripped faster.

Drip... Drip... Drip...

And louder.

DRIP...DRIP...DRIP...

Ethan pulled the covers off and slid out of bed. As soon as his feet touched the floor, he nearly leaped from the shock. Water, cold as ice, covered the floor.

DRIP...DRIP...DRIP...

Maybe there's a leak in the ceiling, he thought. But wait... How could it? It wasn't raining outside.

The dripping came even faster.

DRIP! DRIP! DRIP!

A faint flash of lightning lit the room. Thunder cracked in the distance. The wind began to moan.

Ethan ran across the cold, wet floor to the window and looked out. The full moon shone in a starry sky outside.

He couldn't hear the dripping anymore. The howling wind and pouring rain drowned it out.

Lightning flashed brighter. The thunder cracked louder. They weren't coming from outside. They came from inside the room!

Ethan spun around, water splashing at his feet several inches deep.

Lightning flashed again from the painting on the wall.

The picture was moving, and a terrible storm raged around the ship. Tiny, frantic figures ran around the ship's deck. They tried to secure the ripped and tattered sails. But the storm was so fierce it looked hopeless.

Rain poured into the room, and waves crashed over the picture frame.

A foot of water now covered the floor.

Another wave crashed from the painting, and the cold water rose to Ethan's knees.

He ran to the door, but another wave burst out and knocked him over.

He clung to the dresser and pulled himself up. The water was up to his chest.

Lightning flashed again. The mast on the ship snapped and fell into the angry waves.

The water was now over Ethan's head. He struggled to swim over to his floating bed. Soon, the water would overwhelm the whole room.

Ethan took one last glimpse at the painting. The ship pointed upward, sinking into the dark ocean. Then, the whole painting vanished beneath the water in the room.

Ethan had only a foot of space left. The water was almost to the ceiling.

Then, only eight inches.

Then four.

Ethan took his final breath as the water closed in around him.

With a gasp, Ethan shot up in bed.

The morning sun glowed outside the window.

He got up and hurried over to look at the painting. He saw a little sign on the frame. It said the ship in the painting had sunk in a storm—precisely two hundred years ago that very night.

# 5

# THE THING IN THE JAR

Anna's grandmother asked her to fetch some canned peaches from the cellar. Anna didn't like the cellar. It was old and dark and damp. She scampered down the creaky steps.

She didn't want to be down there for long. Canned food and glass jars filled the dusty shelves. Spider webs hung down from the ceiling.

As she reached for the peaches, Anna's eyes caught sight of something strange.

A pale purple light glowed in the back of a shelf.

Anna pushed aside some canned tomatoes, and there it was.

The light came from an old jar. A heavy layer of dust covered it. The purple light shone faintly

through the dust. It looked like something was moving inside the jar.

Anna's curiosity got the better of her fear.

She reached for the jar and wiped away the thick dust to get a better look.

A dense, purple goo bubbled inside. The jar had no label, so she had no idea what it was.

Inside, the purple goo was swirling. It formed shapes that almost seemed alive.

The glowing purple swirls were hypnotizing, and she couldn't look away.

Her hand seemed to move on its own. In a moment, she twisted the top and removed the lid.

Tendrils of purple mist rose from the goo. The smell was indescribable! She had to try tasting it. She lowered her finger towards the goo.

"Anna!" Shouted her grandmother from up in the kitchen. "Hurry and get those peaches!"

Startled, Anna dropped the jar.

It crashed to the floor and shattered!

A thick purple fog rose from the goo. It filled the cellar with eerie purple light.

Eerie plants twisted and turned in the fog. Their leaves shimmered with an unnatural purple glow. Strange monsters lurked in the mist, like creatures from a nightmare. Some had too many eyes, and others had tentacles.

Then the monsters stopped and slowly turned towards her. Anna was too afraid to move.

The monsters rushed forward with a chorus of alien screeches and growls. Anna's fear turned to terror.

With her heart racing, Anna turned and ran as fast as she could.

She dashed up the stairs.

The sounds of the creatures echoed behind her.

She reached the top and slammed the door shut behind her.

"Anna!" Exclaimed her grandmother. "If you're too afraid of the cellar, I'll just have to go get them myself!"

Anna tried to block the door. Puffs of purple mist crept through the gap at the bottom. But Anna's grandmother was too busy moving Anna aside to notice before opening the cellar door.

# 6
# THE SPECTACLES OF AGATHA HUMPHREYS

My name is Phillip, and I live at 317 Woodfront Ave. It is right across the street from where an old lady named Agatha Humphreys lived.

But not anymore.

She was killed.

And nobody knew about it.

Nobody, that is, except me.

That's because I'm the one that killed her.

But let me explain.

It isn't what you think.

You see, Agatha Humphreys was no ordinary old lady.

She was mean and scary. Her nose was sharp, and her eyes seemed to see through you. She always wore big, round spectacles.

One day, while playing ball, it accidentally went into her yard. I had to get it.

I snuck into her garden, full of weird plants and creepy statues.

I saw the spectacles on a small table. I suddenly wanted to try them on for a moment. I don't know why. It was like they were calling out to me. Like there was something they wanted to show me.

When I put them on, everything changed.

The world turned dark, and I saw things...

Terrible things...

Shadows moved like twisted faces and figures in the corners of my eyes.

I heard this awful whispering but couldn't understand the strange language.

Then, I saw Agatha standing on the porch of the house. But now she wasn't a frail old lady. Now, she was something else, something not human—a creature from a nightmare.

Agatha screeched in rage when she saw the glasses on my face. She raised her twisted, clawed hands and charged toward me.

I turned and dashed away, deeper into the garden. I could hear the heavy thumping of her feet as she dashed down the path behind me.

The plants in the garden now looked twisted and black. Some even had giant bulging mouths and tooth-filled pods. They snapped at me as I ran.

Up ahead was a large, twisted statue of a monster. It had too many arms and legs. I dove and hid behind it.

Then Agatha appeared.

Her sneering face twisted in anger. Her nostrils flared like she was trying to smell the air to know which way I went.

My heart beat so hard I thought it would give my hiding spot away.

I only had a moment to think of a plan. She was right around the corner!

I grabbed a rock and threw it into some toothy plants behind her.

Agatha spun around with a snarl.

As soon as she did, I charged into her from behind. She fell over into one of her plants.

I heard the plants snapping and biting.

I heard her scream.

But I kept running.

I didn't stop until I was back home across the street. I ripped the spectacles off my face and threw them onto the sidewalk. I stomped on them as hard as I could. The glass broke, and the frames bent into a twisted mess.

I ran to my room and looked out the window at Agatha's house. Everything looked normal again.

There was no sign of Agatha.

I never saw her again.

No one did.

I was so scared I never told anyone what happened.

I thought it was over, but one night, things got stranger.

I heard the strange whispers again and saw shadows moving in my room.

It was just a bad dream, but when I woke up in the morning, I still heard the whispers and saw the flickering shadows from the corners of my eyes.

And there, on my dresser top, good as new, were Agatha's spectacles.

# 7
# THE GHOST OF CAMP GREEN LAKE

Dillon was a boy who went to Camp Green Lake for the summer. He loved the trees, the songs, and the campfires.

But he had a problem.

Every night, Dillon wet the bed. When the other boys in his cabin found out, they laughed at him. Dillon felt sad and alone.

One evening, feeling extra sad, Dillon walked alone by the lake. The other boys had been teasing him all day.

The sky was filled with the colors of twilight. He found a driftwood log and sat down. Looking at the rippling water, he tried to forget the teasing.

Dillon kicked at the mud aimlessly and noticed something bright yellow. He grabbed a stick and dug

the yellow thing out. It was an old yo-yo.

"Hey! You found my yo-yo!" said a voice behind him as he wiped the mud away.

It was another boy dressed in a Camp Green Lake uniform. Dillon didn't recognize him. He must be in a different cabin.

"Hi, I'm Jake," the boy said and sat beside him. "I lost that yo-yo in the lake my first year here. But you can keep it."

"Thanks," Dillon said.

It was the first nice thing anyone said to

Dillon all day. It helped him feel a little better. Jake kept talking and telling funny stories, and Dillon soon started laughing.

It was getting late, and it was time to return to the cabins for bed.

Dillon thanked him for making him feel better.

"Good." Jake grinned. "And don't worry about the other boys. I'm sure things will be better for you tomorrow."

Dillon stood and stretched. He was about to ask Jake what cabin he was staying in. But when Dillon turned back, Jake was already gone.

Dillon shrugged. He was sure he would see Jake again later.

After Dillon fell asleep that night, something strange happened in his cabin.

All the boys in the cabin were asleep when the cabin door creaked open.

A ghostly figure of a boy entered.

He rippled like moving water and silently crept over to the sleeping boys.

The mysterious boy's cold, dripping hands reached toward them.

All the boys who teased Dillon started tossing and turning. Horrible nightmares filled their dream with scenes of a dark and watery world.

In the morning, all the other boys were terrified, remembering their awful dreams, and

shocked to discover that each of their beds was soaked.

Embarrassed, they all huddled together. Dillon overheard them talking about the ghostly nightmare.

"It was so real," one boy said, shaking.

"Yeah," another boy muttered. "The cold water, the whispers, his face..."

The other boys didn't tease Dillon like they did every other morning. They all dressed quietly and went to the mess hall for breakfast.

 42

As they stood in line, one of the boys pointed to an old photograph. There were many framed photos.

One for every summer.

The one the boy pointed to was taken many years ago.

"That's him!" the boy whispered to the other. "It's the boy from my nightmare."

The others looked at the photo and nodded in agreement.

They'd all seen him.

Dillon looked at the photo, too.

It was Jake.

And in his hand was the yo-yo.

Jake drowned in the lake many years ago.

# 8
# FIONA'S FAREWELL

Fiona was usually a cheerful girl. She lived in a big, creaky house with her family. But she was sad because they were moving soon. It was the night of their big farewell party.

The house was buzzing with people, music, and laughter. Fiona loved seeing her friends one last time before saying goodbye. But then she noticed a strange woman staring at her.

The woman wore a long, old-fashioned dress. Nobody seemed to know her or talk to her.

Every time Fiona went into a different room, the strange lady was there waiting. She wouldn't stop staring at Fiona.

The woman made Fiona feel nervous. She seemed sad somehow, and Fiona felt sorry for her. She didn't know why.

Curious, Fiona approached her.

"Hi, I'm Fiona," she said with a smile. "Are you ok?"

The woman looked down sadly and whispered, "This house has a secret."

Fiona's smile faded.

"This house is cursed," the woman whispered and leaned closer.

"Long ago," the woman continued, "a family vanished. It happened on the night before they planned to leave the house."

Fiona took a nervous step back, "But... tonight's the night before we plan to leave."

"The house won't let you," the strange woman

whispered. "It will trap your spirits here forever."

Fiona felt a chill.

She wasn't sure what to think.

Was the woman just making up a story to scare her?

The woman shook her head, "I'm not making up a story, but you should be scared. You must believe me."

Fiona gasped. Had the woman read her thoughts?

The strange woman's eyes were dark and severe. She reached out and handed Fiona a folded piece of paper.

Fiona opened it up. Inside, it said:

Here is the secret.

If you walk up the stairs, counting each step out loud, you can leave. But your family will be trapped forever.

If you walk up the stairs backward, counting each step out loud, your family can leave. But you will be trapped here forever.

But you must reach the top before midnight. If you don't, there will be no hope for any of you.

You must make a choice.

Don't make the wrong one!

Fiona looked up when she finished reading, but the strange woman was gone.

The party continued.

Fiona couldn't stop thinking about the

woman's words. The clock ticked louder in her ears.

It was almost midnight!

Fiona read the note over and over. She wanted to tell her parents, but there wasn't time.

She looked at the clock on the wall—only a minute left!

The house felt colder. She saw shadows flickering in the corners of the room. They looked like sad people dressed in old-fashioned clothes.

Is this the curse? She thought.

The clock began to strike!

Suddenly, the house went dark.

Fiona heard whispers and felt a cold wind.

'Trapped forever...'

The clock struck again!

She had to make a choice.

The chimes of the clock were sounding!

Fiona took a deep breath and started up the stairs.

# 9
# THE TRUNK
# OF DOOM

Mason loved comic books. He had so many that they were all over his room. One day, he was walking down the street carrying a big stack of old comics. His friend had just given them all to him. There were so many that he could hardly carry them.

While struggling with his comics, he saw a strange man in an alley. The tall man wore a heavy black overcoat. His dusty black hat shadowed his face.

The man held out an old trunk.

"You should take this," the man said. "Its previous owner no longer needs it."

Mason thought it would be perfect for his comics. So, he thanked the mysterious man and carried the trunk home. The trunk was big enough

to hold all his comic books.

That night, something spooky happened.

Mason heard a creepy, croaking voice coming from the dark shadows of his room.

"Doom!" it said.

"Doom!"

Over and over.

Mason loved reading scary comics. But this wasn't a comic. This was real. Terrified, his mind was full of wild ideas about what it could be.

Was it a monster?

A ghost?

A specter of ultimate evil?

"Doom!" croaked the voice. "DOOOOOM!"

Mason jumped out of bed and turned on the light.

The voice fell silent.

Mason slept with the light on all night.

The following day, he checked the old trunk. Was it haunted?

He pulled out all the comic books but didn't find anything.

Throughout school, he could hear the creepy voice repeating "Doom!" in his head. He was sure something horrible was going to happen.

But nothing did.

That night, he emptied the trunk and placed it on the foot of his bed.

Then he turned off the light, sat at the head of the bed, and waited.

He began to drift off when the voice started to sound.

"DOOM! DOOM! DOOM!" the harsh voice croaked.

Now Mason was sure it was coming from the trunk.

Mason rushed to the light and turned it on.

Mason pulled the comic books out of the trunk and searched it again. This time, he noticed a narrow gap in the bottom edge. The trunk must have a false bottom hiding a secret compartment. What could be hidden there? A lost treasure? Some secret papers and maps? The bones of an evil sorcerer whose ghost haunted the trunk?

Mason grabbed a pair of scissors and stuck them into the gap. Nervously, he pried open the bottom.

Suddenly, with the loudest "DOOM!" of all, something jumped out of the compartment right at Mason.

It was a tiny green frog that landed on Mason's lap.

Its neck swelled with air.

"Doom!" It croaked. "Doom!"

Mason laughed. It was just a little frog. Maybe his mom would let him keep it as a pet, and he would name it Doom.

In an instant, the air seemed to shimmer as the space around Mason stretched and warped. Everything around him grew colossal while he shrank down.

"Doom!" Croaked the frog on the bed.

"Doom!" Cried the new frog next to it.

A shadowy figure appeared in the room. The figure's hand reached out and made a strange gesture. The frogs flew into the trunk. The secret compartment clicked closed, and the Trunk snapped shut.

The man with the black hat stepped out of the shadows and took the trunk.

Its previous owner wouldn't be needing it any longer.

# 10
# THE DOOR IN THE DARK CORNER

One night, Amelia heard a strange sound and woke up. It was like many voices whispering from the dark corner of her room. She sat up in bed but couldn't see much in the dark.

She tried to ignore them, but the whispers grew louder.

"Who's there?" Amelia asked, but no one answered. She felt scared, but she decided to find out who was whispering.

She crept to the sound, gripping her teddy bear for courage.

The whispers stopped.

She saw nothing but shadows.

Then, the wall shimmered like water, and Amelia saw a door appear.

Slowly, the door began to swing open.

On the other side, she saw a strange, magical world.

Stars danced and spun in circles in the sky. Strange flowers bloomed in a wide clearing surrounded by trees she'd never seen before. A group of friendly children ran and played in the soft grass. They smiled and waved when they saw Amelia standing in the doorway.

"Come and play with us," they shouted.

Something didn't feel right. Amelia felt

nervous. She didn't know why.

But Amelia wanted to see more of the magical world.

As she went through the door, her teddy bear fell to the ground. It couldn't come through with her. It's ok, she thought. I can always get him when I come back.

Amelia ran around and played games with the children.

They wanted to take her further into the trees. They said there was a special place. It was deeper in the woods. It was where they played their special game.

Amelia didn't know. She might never find her way back if she lost sight of the door.

The children laughed and said she was being silly. They said she would always be safe in their magical world. Amelia knew she should get back to her room.

The children told her she could come to play with them again tomorrow night.

Amelia returned through the door, picked up her teddy bear, and got into bed. In the morning, the door was gone. Amelia thought about telling her friends at school or her parents. But she didn't. They would never believe her.

She was excited to see if the door would appear again the next night. She went to bed and waited, but she fell asleep. She woke up to hear her friends whispering, "Come play with us." She sat up and saw the door appear again in the corner.

She went through the door and played with the children. Again, the children wanted her to go deeper into the woods. She said no. They seemed sad but continued playing with her near the door anyway.

The third night, the door appeared again. Amelia got up and went through.

When the children begged her to play their special game this time, she gave in. Her friends were so nice, and she was sure they would help her find her way back if needed.

Amelia followed the children deeper into the magical forest. She was excited to play their special game. They reached a place with a huge stone carved with strange swirling patterns. The air around it sparkled with tiny lights.

"Here's where we play our special game," one child said.

"The game is simple," another child explained. "First, everyone puts their hand on the stone."

The children gathered around and placed their hands on the stone. Excited to play this new game, Amelia reached out and touched the stone, too.

"Now," said another child, "when the lights go out, we all race to your door!"

"The first one to go through," said another,

"wins the prize!"

"What prize?" Amelia asked with excitement.

The children all turned toward Amelia and smiled.

Wide, creepy smiles.

The lights around the stone began to fade. As they did, all the children started to change. They turned into dark, shadowy children. Their eyes grew wide and blank. When they smiled, their mouths were filled with sharp teeth.

"Whoever goes through your door first gets

to become YOU!" one of the shadow children said.

The lights around the stone kept growing fainter and fainter.

"FOREVER!" cheered all the shadow children together.

"But rules are rules," another shadow child said. "We have to give you a count of ten head start."

With those last words, the lights went out.

Amelia was so shocked she just stood there. She didn't know what to say.

"TEN!" the shadow children shouted together.

"NINE!"

"EIGHT!"

Amelia's heart pounded with fear.

"SEVEN!"

The game was a race for her own life!

"SIX!"

Amelia had to move. She was running out of time! She turned and sprinted through the trees.

"FIVE!"

Amelia ran as fast as she could but didn't know her way through the trees. Everything had turned dark and creepy. The stars had gone out. The trees were black and bare, like a maze that twisted and turned around her.

"FOUR!" shouted the shadow children.

The branches reached out like hands, trying to hold Amelia back.

"THREE!"

Amelia couldn't find the path back to her door.

"TWO!"

Amelia was lost.

"ONE!"

That was it. Amelia lost her head start.

"LET'S GO!" the shadow children shouted somewhere behind her.

The shadow children were getting closer. Their laughter echoed through the trees, eerie and chilling. Amelia tried to run faster, but it was no use.

Then she spotted them. She was going in the wrong direction. She turned, but they were now all ahead of her. They were pulling and grabbing each other. They would do anything to be the winner.

It was her only chance.

Amelia tried to run faster.

There it was: her door!

But the familiar clearing was now dark. The soft grass was gone. Now it was filled with patches of dirt, dead weeds, and briars.

One of the shadow children tried to knock her down as she ran past. She dodged out of the way. Then she ran past another and another.

Suddenly, she stumbled in the thick weeds and fell to the ground.

She hurried to get up, but she was too late.

Just inside the door, she saw HERSELF standing in HER room holding HER teddy bear.

"Don't worry," the new Amelia said with a grin. "I'll take good care of him. Have fun playing your games!"

The new Amelia waved goodbye to all her friends and shut the door.

# 11
# RUNNING SHORT

Raymond was a boy who loved to run. More than anything, he wanted to win the big race at school. One sunny afternoon, he was talking to his friend Mike.

"I've been practicing," Raymond said excitedly. "I'm pretty fast, but I wish I could run as fast as the wind. I'd do anything to win!"

A tall man, who stood in the shade of a nearby tree, overheard him. The man wore a black coat and a black hat that shadowed his face.

"Be careful what you wish for," said the man in a low voice. "But I'm sure it will be a race you will never forget."

A chill ran down Raymond's spine. Before he could say anything, the man turned and disappeared around a corner.

Later, at home, Raymond found a new pair of running shorts on his bed. They were shiny and felt

unusually smooth.

"Thanks for the new shorts, Mom," he told her at dinner. "I'm going to wear them for the race tomorrow."

"New shorts?" His mom asked, confused.

"The shorts I found in my room," he said.

His mom frowned and then shrugged. "I guess I must have forgotten buying them for you. But I'm glad you like them."

The next morning, Raymond wore the new shorts. They fit perfectly, and he felt they were made just for him.

"Ready, set, go!" The race started, and Raymond began to run with all his might.

As he picked up speed, Raymond noticed something strange.

He ran faster than ever before!

I'm like the wind! He thought. A thrill of excitement ran through him.

But then, Raymond began to feel lighter, almost weightless.

He looked down at his hands in horror. They were fading away!

What's happening to me!?

Despite his fear, Raymond kept running. He was far ahead of the others now.

The finish line was in sight, even though there was almost nothing left of Raymond to be seen.

I'm disappearing, he realized in terror!

He caught a glimpse of the strange man with the black hat. He was watching Raymond from the back of the crowd, waiting near the finish line.

But Raymond was almost to the end!

Just steps from the finish line, the rest of Raymond faded away. Only his clothes were left.

First, his shoes thumped to the ground.

Then, his shirt.

Finally, Raymond's underpants and running shorts fell to the ground, just short of the finish line.

# 12
# THE WRONG BUS

Scarlett was the only one left on the bus. It was just her and the bus driver.

But then a strange-looking man got on.

He was carrying an odd-shaped paper bag.

The man sat a few seats away from Scarlett. He looked around nervously, holding his bag tightly.

The bus started moving, and Scarlett looked out the window, watching the world go by.

The man kept looking around.

First, he looked nervously out the windows.

Then he looked nervously down at his bag.

Then he looked nervously over at Scarlett.

Finally, he stood up and approached

Scarlett with his bag.

"I think something's wrong," he said to Scarlett in a cold whisper.

Then he set his bag down on the seat across from Scarlett and sat next to it.

He leaned over and spoke to Scarlett again, "I think we're on the wrong bus."

Scarlett frowned, "What do you mean?"

"Look out the windows," he said and pointed.

Scarlett looked outside.

It was getting darker, but it didn't seem that strange to Scarlett. It was almost dinner time.

Scarlett smiled at the man. "Don't worry," she said, trying to sound cheerful. "I'm sure my stop is coming soon."

Nervously, the man pulled out a package of cookies from his paper bag. He ate one to calm his nerves and offered one to Scarlett.

"No, thank you," Scarlett said, even though she was very hungry. "It's almost dinner time, and my parents wouldn't be happy if I spoiled it."

A few minutes passed, and the scenery outside was getting spookier.

The trees looked like twisted monsters, and the sky turned a deep, eerie red. Sometimes, their branches scraped against the bus's roof.

But that didn't bother Scarlett.

What bothered her was the strange man.

He was shaking his head vigorously.

"No," he whispered to himself. "No, no, no. This can't be the right bus."

The man stood and moved to the front of the bus to speak to the driver.

The driver seemed to be in a trance. He wouldn't answer or stop the bus.

The man grew more and more scared.

He tried to open a window, but it was stuck.

He tried another, and it, too, was stuck.

He tried another and another.

He pushed the latch for the emergency door in the back. It wouldn't open.

Scarlett was beginning to get very worried.

Suddenly, the bus slowed to a stop, and the door opened.

The strange man rushed out, hoping to find a way back home.

Outside was a dark, sinister forest. Beneath the branches was a dirt path leading into the woods.

Scarlett followed the man out of the bus.

Several monstrous shapes were moving toward them in the darkness.

They hurried down the path. Their footsteps thumping louder and louder.

The man was terrified.

He grabbed Scarlett's hand. He wanted to pull her back to the safety of the bus.

But the bus doors closed, and it drove away.

"Run," the man shouted to Scarlett.

He tried to pull her with him, but she held back.

The man tried to let go of Scarlett's hand,

but her grip was too tight.

Scarlett smiled up at him. "It's okay. This is my stop."

The man stared at Scarlett in horror. He tried to pull free, but her grip was unnaturally strong. Her face was beginning to change.

"That's my family waiting for us," said Scarlet. "I told you. It's almost dinner time."

# 13
# MS. FORTUNE

A group of children arrived at their classroom. They thought it would be a normal day. Then they learned their teacher, Mrs. Jenkins, had mysteriously disappeared. Standing at the front of the room was their new substitute teacher, Ms. Fortune.

Ms. Fortune was tall and thin. She had mean, icy blue eyes and a voice that sent shivers down your spine. Her smile seemed more like a snarl, and she moved like a shadow across the room.

The children felt uneasy around her.

Strange things began to happen that day.

Emily, who was scared of spiders, opened her desk to pull out a pencil. Hundreds of spiders swarmed out all over her. She screamed and slammed the desk shut. Ms. Fortune glared at Emily. But when she came and opened the desk, the spiders were gone.

Later, Tom got locked in the classroom closet.

He was terrified of small spaces. Tom screamed and banged on the door, but it wouldn't open. The other children tried to open the door, but it wouldn't budge.

Ms. Fortune walked over with an evil grin and opened it easily. "It was never locked," she said, her voice cold.

Lily was afraid of snakes. At lunch, she opened her bag, reached in, and pulled out a slithering snake! She screamed and threw it to the ground. But when Ms. Fortune stormed over, the only thing on the ground was a banana.

Later that afternoon, the lights flickered and went out. The classroom plunged into darkness. It was so deep that even the sunlight from the windows vanished. Many of the children screamed. When the lights came back. Ms. Fortune was standing in the front of the room, grinning evilly.

When another teacher came into the room. Ms. Fortune seemed to change somehow. Her voice became sweet, and her eyes sparkled kindly. She seemed like the nicest teacher in the world. But as soon as the other teacher left, she changed into her nasty old self.

And that was just on the first day! Each day, things became worse.

A curious boy, Barry, stumbled upon an old book in the library. It was a book about monsters and magic. As he read, he realized Ms. Fortune matched the description of a creature called a 'Nightmare Hag.' She fed on the fear of children and brought misfortune wherever she went.

He learned a secret about how to get rid of a nightmare hag. They had to trick her into writing her name with a black pen. If she did, she would get trapped in the pen!

Barry told Richard about his plan, and the next day, they worked together.

During class, Barry and Richard began arguing.

Ms. Fortune rushed over and glared at them.

"You will work quietly, or you will be punished."

"Sorry, Ms. Fortune," mumbled Richard.

"Yes, we were just arguing about how to spell your name," said Barry.

Barry held up his paper. It said, "Ms. Fertshoon."

Richard held up his paper. It said, "Ms. Fartshun."

Ms. Fortune glared furiously at the horrible misspellings. She snatched the pen from Barry's hand and scribbled on the paper.

"M-S F-O-R-T-U-N-E," she snarled, speaking the letters as she wrote. "That is how you—" But her words were cut short.

As soon as she finished writing, she began to screech! Ms. Fortune began turning into a cloud of inky black smoke. The smoke poured into the pen with an awful whoosh.

Ms. Fortune was gone.

The children cheered!

They had trapped the nightmare hag! But Barry knew he had to be careful with the pen. A pen with a nightmare hag trapped in it could only write horrible stories. And if the ink ever ran out, the nightmare hag would be set free.

Barry took the pen home and hid it someplace where he hoped no one would ever find it.

## Congratulations, brave reader!

You've made it through all 13 terrifying tales from

# THE FORBIDDEN LIBRARY.

It takes real courage to face these stories,
and you did it! But *BEWARE*—these stories have
a way of sticking with you... and who knows
what might happen next!

**If you enjoyed the frightful fun, please leave a
review on Amazon and tell me which story was your
favorite.**

And stay tuned—Volume 2 is creeping closer!
You never know... you might find yourself
or someone you know caught in the next
13 spine-chilling stories!

Until then, watch your back and remember:
some stories are better left *UNTOLD*...

Esau C. Helbelcher, the undisputed scribe of the sinister and illustrator of the inexplicable, returns with his latest masterpiece, "The Forbidden Library: Volume 1, 13 Scary Stories that Should NEVER be Told," to once again captivate and frighten readers of all ages.

He is often asked where he gets the inspiration for such spine-chilling stories. He responds that such stories just come to him. He sits at his desk late at night and writes by the light of a single candle using an old, black pen he found years ago. When he does, the stories spring into his mind, almost like someone whispering the words in his ear.

Mr. Helbelcher dives headfirst into the abyss of fear, emerging with tales that linger long after turning the final page. On the other hand, Achelles Ubreech's "The Decay of Green House" and "The Tale of the Boegrush" only skim the surface of the dark waters of fright, while Helbelcher's stories pull you under, immersing you entirely in the depths of terror.

When he's not writing or illustrating his stories, Esau enjoys perfecting his prize-winning gingerbread recipe, training garden snails how to leave insulting limericks about Mr. Ubreech in their slime trails on his doorstep, and gobbling up as many marshmallows as he pleases.

## More Great Books by
# Esau C. Helbelcher!
## The Charming Stubileys

From A to Z, the Stubileys find themselves in increasingly bizarre predicaments, with each whimsical poem delivering a surprising spooky twist! Discover the grim fates of these mischievous children with captivating yet chilling illustrations.

## Waiting in the Darkness

The sun has set.
The lights are out.
You think you're alone in your room.
Then a branch scrapes against your window.
It's just the wind, you think, or is it...
Maybe something's out there
Something lurking just out of sight...
Are you brave enough to face the things
*Waiting in the Darkness?*

You could also try these books by
# Achelles Ubreech
(But just to confirm how much better Mr. Helbelcher's books are!)

## The Decay of Green House

The decrepit mansion looms before you in the moonlight.
The eerie corridors and silent chambers of Green House beckon.
Do you dare enter and explore its depths?
Maybe you will be the one to
unravel its secrets...
Maybe you will discover the
treasure concealed within its walls...

## The Tale of the Boegrush

Something has begun to emerge from the murky depths of the swamp. Something that leaves a trail of destruction in its wake. Could it really be the monstrous creature spoken of in legend?
Maybe there's more than one secret lurking in the shadowy depths of the ancient swamp.
Maybe you have the courage to open the book and discover the truth for yourself...

Made in United States
North Haven, CT
20 April 2025

68128854R00046